'Long live King Solomon!' shouted all the people.

Solomon was the new king of Israel. He wanted to be a good king like his father, David.

Solomon knew that when his father had obeyed God everything went well. So he made up his mind that he would be the kind of king who obeyed God, too.

God was pleased that Solomon had decided to obey him. He spoke to Solomon in a dream.

'What would you like from me as a special present?' God said. 'You can have whatever you ask for.'

golden temple

Story by Penny Frank

Illustrated by Tony Morris

THE LION
STORY BIBLE

20

OXFORD · BATAVIA · SYDNEY

Τhe Bible tells us
how God chose the Israelites to be his
special people. He made them a
promise that he would always love
and care for them. But they must
obey him.
In this story, David's son Solomon
becomes king when David dies.
Solomon has seen that the way to
serve God is to obey and trust him.
You can find the story in your own
Bible, in the first book of Kings,
chapters 3 to 10.

Copyright © 1987 Lion Publishing

Published by
Lion Publishing plc
Sandy Lane West, Littlemore, Oxford, England
ISBN 0 85648 745 7
Lion Publishing Corporation
1705 Hubbard Avenue, Batavia,
Illinois 60510, USA
ISBN 0 85648 745 7
Albatross Books Pty Ltd
PO Box 320, Sutherland, NSW 2232, Australia
ISBN 0 86760 529 4

First edition 1987
Reprinted 1988

Printed in Yugoslavia
Bound in Great Britain

**British Library Cataloguing in
Publication Data**

Frank, Penny
  Solomon's golden temple. - (The Lion
  Story Bible; 20)
  1. Solomon *King of Israel* - Juvenile
  literature
  I. Title   II. Morris, Tony, *1938 Aug 2-*
  222'.530924   BS580.S6

ISBN 0-85648-745-7

**Library of Congress Cataloging in
Publication Data**

Frank, Penny.
  Solomon's golden temple.
  (The Lion Story Bible; 20)
  1. Solomon, King of Israel—Juvenile
  literature. 2. Palestine—Kings and
  rulers—Biography—Juvenile literature.
  3. Temple of Jerusalem (Jerusalem)—
  Juvenile literature. 4. Bible stories,
  English—O.T. Kings, 1st. [1. Solomon,
  King of Israel. 2. Bible stories—O.T.] I.
  Morris, Tony, ill. II. Title. III. Series:
  Frank, Penny. Lion Story Bible; 20.
  BS580.S6F68 1987   222'.5309505
  86-18522
  ISBN 0-85648-745-7

'What I really need,' said Solomon, 'is wisdom. I don't see how I can make a good job of being king unless you make me wise.'

God was pleased with Solomon's answer.

'I will give you wisdom,' he said, 'and fame and riches, too.'

God made Solomon very wise. All the Israelites came with their problems to the king, because he had good answers.

Even people from other lands came. They heard that God had made Solomon very rich and very wise.

One day the queen of Sheba came on a long journey to visit Solomon.

She asked him questions. She listened to his answers.

She looked at his beautiful palace and all his riches.

'They told me how rich you are,' she said to Solomon. 'They told me you are very wise. I thought I would be disappointed when I saw what you were really like. But now I know that you are twice as magnificent as they told me.'

Solomon looked around his land.

When the Israelites had first come to the land they had lived in tents.

Now they had houses to live in, and strong walled cities.

But there was no house for God.

'We ought to build God a beautiful house,' said Solomon, 'the temple my father, King David, planned.

'It will be the most beautiful temple ever built. And inside it we will keep the special box which holds God's laws, to remind us of his promises.'

So Solomon set to work.

'We will make it from stone, wood and gold,' said Solomon. 'And we will use the very best workmen.'

Solomon sent a message to the king of
Tyre.

'I'm building a temple for God,' he
said. 'Please send me some of your
beautiful cedar trees, so that the temple
can be really special.'

Solomon sent for the men who were good at working in stone and wood and gold.

'This is going to be a special building for God,' he said. 'We must not have a lot of noise and shouting while it is being made. Do all the work here in the quarry. Then carry the stones to the temple and put them together.'

They all worked hard for a very long time. The house of God was not big, like a cathedral, but it was very beautiful. And there was room all around it for the people to come.

17

At last it was finished. They could bring the special box into the new temple.

It had its own room. The walls were covered in gold.

When Solomon and the people saw the finished temple, they knew it was very beautiful.

It was the very best they could build.

19

Solomon called the people together.

'The temple is finished,' he said. 'The special box is inside. We must thank God for helping us to build the temple.'

So Solomon and the people prayed.

'We know that you are far too great to live in one place on earth,' they said. 'But please make the temple a very special place where we know you are near us.'

Suddenly a bright, dazzling light filled the temple. They knew that God had heard their prayer.

God had given his people a great and
wise king.

As they went to worship God at his
beautiful temple, they knew that the city
of Jerusalem was now a very special
place. God himself was there with them.

The Lion Story Bible is made up of 52 individual stories for young readers, building up an understanding of the Bible as one story — God's story — a story for all time and all people.

The Old Testament section (numbers 1–30) tells the story of a great nation — God's chosen people, the Israelites — and God's love and care for them through good times and bad. The stories are about people who knew and trusted God. From this nation came one special person, Jesus Christ, sent by God to save all people everywhere.

The story of King Solomon is told in the Old Testament history book, 1 Kings, chapters 1–11. The visit of the Queen of Sheba is in chapter 10; the building and dedication of the temple in chapters 6–8.

King David's many battles ensured a reign of peace and prosperity for his son, Solomon. Never again would the kingdom of Israel be so great; never again would the twelve clans descended from Jacob's sons be united under one king.

King Solomon was famous for his wisdom. He wrote 3,000 proverbs. Some of these, with the other wise sayings he collected, are in the Bible book of Proverbs.

The fabulous temple he built in Jerusalem lasted for about 350 years. Then, sadly, it was destroyed by the Babylonian King Nebuchadnezzar.

The next story in this series, number 21: *Elijah asks for bread*, belongs to the time after the nation had split in two. But God still cared about his people.